CW01475925

Contents

Tick off the ones you've done! ✓

Colouring

8

10

14

16

20

22

26

28

32

34

38

40

42

44

48

52

54

58

60

64

66

68

72

74

78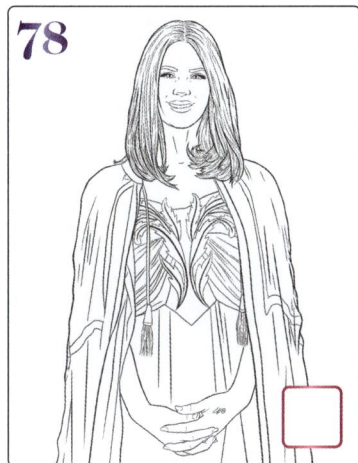

Illustrations Kym Winters

WORLD: MEET LIZZY GRANT

Born Elizabeth Woolridge Grant on 21 June 1985, Lana's childhood would form the cinematic backdrop of her artistry in the years to come. She grew up in Upstate New York in a well-off Catholic family before attending boarding school as a teenager, giving her early inspiration for later beloved themes of spirituality and Americana.

A DARK YOUTH

Lana struggled with the concept of death from a young age. As a teen, she was moved to a strict boarding school in an effort to curb her alcohol abuse. She also dabbled with drugs, but eventually got sober after a stint in rehab. This distressing early experience of addiction later inspired several recurring themes in her songwriting, such as substance abuse, mental health and loneliness.

HER FIRST SIX CHORDS

During a year spent waitressing while staying with family in Long Island, Lana's uncle taught her how to play guitar. These formative lessons – apparently just "six basic chords" – would become the foundation for her music. Lana realised that she "could probably write a million songs" with these first few chords, so an idle hobby became a career path.

BECOMING LANA DEL REY

Before she was Lana, she was Lizzy. In a 2011 interview with British *Vogue*, Lana explained that she wanted to find a stage name that she "could shape the music towards", and was influenced by trips to Miami. 'Lana' is a loose homage to Lana Turner, a Hollywood pin-up girl and actress, while 'Del Rey' was a classic Brazilian Ford car. "Lana Del Rey reminded us of the glamour of the seaside," she explained. "It sounded gorgeous coming off the tip of the tongue."

BEFORE THE BREAKTHROUGH

In Lana's early career, she worked on a number of projects that helped her settle in on her ultimate artistic form. These included EPs, self-released songs, and her very first studio album, *Lana Del Ray* (rather than Rey), which was taken off the market shortly after release due to funding issues. Much of her early work was produced while she was living in a trailer park in New Jersey, with the independent label 5 Points Records, until she moved on to another label and eventually bought the masters.

INSPIRING AN INSPIRATION

Lana has created a distinct and deeply influential artistry – herself influenced by a love of American culture, tragedy and romance. She draws from old-school Hollywood, classic rock, jazz, and beat poets. She has often cited her influences explicitly, from the self-styled "gangster Nancy Sinatra" in her early career to a specific split-second of a Harry Nilsson song being referenced in 'Did You Know That There's a Tunnel Under Ocean Blvd'.

BORN TO DIE

Lana's breakthrough came with the seminal *Born to Die*. It is widely considered a modern masterpiece – despite an initially bewildered reception from critics, the album has since been described as ahead of its time. Forgoing the typical hyper-cheer of 2010s pop, *Born to Die*'s sound was sorrowful, melodramatic and steady. With the orchestral trap-hop production, piercing portrayal of addiction, psychosexual relationships and cinematic Americana, Lana secured her cult status with this industry-impacting album.

THE LANA LOOK

Much like her music, Lana's fashion has been heavily influenced by her love of nostalgia, American culture and a sardonic glamour. From the Tumblr-era floral headbands of 2012, soft-girl sultry smokey eyes, the lyrical "red dress" she slips on and off across her albums, to the Jackie Kennedy homage in 'National Anthem', her aesthetic has always been defined by knowing nods to key eras.

THE LANA CINEMATIC UNIVERSE

Lana's music has always had a cinematic quality, so it's little surprise that Hollywood has come calling. She has lent her skills to the silver screen several times over the years, providing soundtrack singles for several films. From the fittingly Art Deco ballad 'Young and Beautiful' on *The Great Gatsby* and her mournful rendition of 'Once Upon a Dream' for *Maleficent*, to the feisty collab 'Don't Call Me Angel' with Ariana Grande and Miley Cyrus for *Charlie's Angels*, Lana's atmospheric music is a natural fit for the big screen.

THE CHURCH OF LANA

Lana's religious upbringing was formative: her fascination with God and spirituality is evident in her song themes and writing – indeed, *Did You Know...* even includes an excerpt from a sermon. Her exact beliefs don't appear to be strictly traditional; she's also been known to use psychics and once said, "My approach to religion is like my approach to music, I take what I want and I leave the rest."

ULTRAVIOLENCE

Lana released *Ultraviolence* in 2014. Growing on the success of *Born to Die*, this record was praised by critics and fans for its atmospheric, gauzy sound and thematic cohesion. Once again exploring sexual power, loneliness and addiction through ethereal yet piercing lyrics, Lana uses a variety of characters to delve into new perspectives.

A FREEWHEELING SONGWRITING STYLE

Although Lana's songwriting has evolved over the course of her career, it has retained the core DNA that makes a line instantly identifiable as a Lana lyric. They are woozy yet skewering, anguished yet assured, specific and cinematic. She returns again and again to Americana, to violence, to melancholy, sex and soulful fatalism. In interviews, Lana has spoken about how she mostly writes in her car, recording herself while driving so she can sing ideas as they come to her.

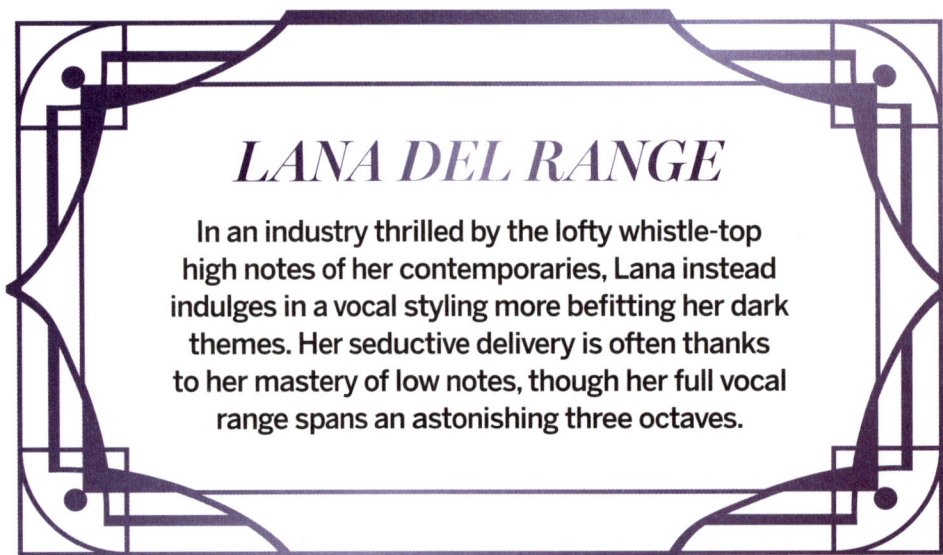

LANA DEL RANGE

In an industry thrilled by the lofty whistle-top high notes of her contemporaries, Lana instead indulges in a vocal styling more befitting her dark themes. Her seductive delivery is often thanks to her mastery of low notes, though her full vocal range spans an astonishing three octaves.

HONEYMOON

A return to the cinematic grandeur of *Born to Die*, Lana's 2015 release, *Honeymoon*, arrived to much fanfare not long after *Ultraviolence*. She floats through the album, at home in the persona of a wistful tortured romantic, with fans and critics praising the record's timelessness. This record also includes Lana's would-be Bond theme: '24'. The song was considered for *Spectre*, but the producers went for 'Writing's on the Wall' by Sam Smith instead.

BORN TO DIRECT

One of the reasons that Lana's work is so singularly identifiable is that she has had a huge role in managing her music's accompanying aesthetic. By directing the majority of her music videos, she has curated a visual identity for her back catalogue, from the launchpad viral 'Video Games' to the surrealist short film *Tropico*.

LUST FOR LIFE

Lana's all-star 2017 album featured some of her biggest collaborations. *Lust for Life* has The Weeknd, Stevie Nicks and A$AP Rocky among others to usher in a hip-hop and soft rock-tinged undercurrent to her usual atmospheric sound. Once again, Lana establishes herself as a true American storyteller, with *Lust for Life* dancing on the Hollywood sign and driving a 'White Mustang'.

THE UNLIKELY HOBBIES OF A POP STAR

In her spare time, Lana has a host of hobbies you might expect of a world famous musician: she's regularly spotted at concerts, theatres, and visiting high-profile restaurants and gyms. What you might not expect is that she is also a passionate Liverpool FC supporter, dabbled in "casting spells", and has even worked a shift in a Waffle House restaurant. Now that's range!

LANA FEAT. HER FAVOURITE COLLABORATORS

Lana's body of work has been enriched by a surprising volume and variety of artists. Though she has a sprawling collaborators list – an eclectic mix of Taylor Swift, Jon Batiste, Father John Misty and more – she seems to have a select few on speed dial for returning projects, including The Weeknd and Jack Antonoff.

LANA LIVE

To go to a Lana Del Rey concert is to immerse yourself in the worlds she conjures. Her live shows evoke the atmospheric Americana of her albums, with escapism woven through her ethereal sets: think flower swings, scores of brides, riding in on Harley-Davidsons and hitting a vape at a vanity mirror. Above all, it's her unique lyrics and mesmerising vocals that are centre stage.

NORMAN FUCKING ROCKWELL!

One of Lana's undeniable talents is parsing together cultural references while remaining timeless: her 2019 album *Norman Fucking Rockwell!* is a masterclass in this. Rockwell, John Lennon, Neil Young, Joni Mitchell and others are all paid homage to in this Americana-laced soft-rock success that topped charts and 'Best Album of the Year' lists worldwide.

CREATING A LANA MASTERPIECE

Contemporary and close collaborator Jon Batiste described Lana's song-crafting process as "like a beast", where she'll divine together abstract narrative threads, and build a song from those. Producer Rick Nowels noted how "effortlessly" she can pull together lyrics, and even that when recording vocals she "does not need many takes" to land on the final version.

BEYOND LYRICS: LANA'S POETRY

Lana's skill in songwriting has set her apart from her contemporaries, earning her the unofficial title "poet of a generation" in the industry. It's fitting then that Lana published a collection of poems, *Violet Bent Backwards over the Grass*, in 2020. She said the process felt very different and more "free form" than her songwriting, and the book secured a Top 5 spot on the *New York Times* Bestseller list.

CHEMTRAILS OVER THE COUNTRY CLUB

In what would be her first of two 2021 albums, *Chemtrails...* took on a more folksy feel, though it remains rooted in Lana's ubiquitous hazy, scenic sound. The record carries less "LA menace" as Lana put it, instead pursuing a "lighter emotional vulnerability". Alongside the autobiographical notes, Lana explores stories inspired by her close female friends. It's these friends that grace the album's 1950s-esque cover photo.

THE GRANTS

Lana has publicly addressed her relationship with her family through her songs, as in 'The Grants', 'A&W', and 'Wildflower Wildfire', often pointing to a perhaps strained maternal relationship. She is, however, very close with her siblings. Indeed, her younger sister Caroline (aka 'Chuck', pictured right) is a photographer, and has collaborated with Lana on several projects.

A CAREER SPENT GIVING BACK

As her career has gone on, Lana has used her platform for a number of good causes. She's known for donating proceeds of her projects to charities, once stating that "every dollar" she makes in ticket sales goes back to the town she performed in. Beyond financial support, Lana has spent years working in homelessness and addiction outreach.

BLUE BANISTERS

Released just seven months after *Chemtrails over the Country Club*, *Blue Banisters* surprised fans. Lana released this album as an introspective, observational record in defence of what she felt were accusations about her art's authenticity and themes. She even said to *Rolling Stone*, "I didn't want anyone to listen to it". Perhaps unfortunately for her then, the album was received by its smaller audience as a delicately defiant success.

HER BEST EVER LOOKS

Whether on the red carpet or on stage, Lana's retro-glam looks have dazzled fans. Iconic moments include her vixen red lip on her controversial nude 2012 *GQ* magazine cover, the bejewelled Dolce & Gabbana baby blue custom dress she wore draped on a piano at Coachella 2024, and of course this extravagantly ethereal woodland gauze McQueen look from the 2024 Met Gala.

MEET THE LANITAS

'Lanitas' (or sometimes 'Lanatics') is the self-given title to hardcore Lana fans. This tongue-in-cheek name might sound like hyperbole, but Lana has admitted in interviews that she often recognises individual fans from tour to tour. Her interactions with them are often very personal, with her handwriting lyrics for tattoos, following them on Instagram and even kissing them.

In Daddy we trust

DID YOU KNOW THAT THERE'S A TUNNEL UNDER OCEAN BLVD

Did You Know... was released in 2023, and was widely considered one of the best records of the year. The beguiling title is a reference to a real disused tunnel, and acts as a metaphor for the album's overarching theme of the fear of being forgotten. Legacy presents itself as a core concern of Lana's, with key tracks including the eponymous single, 'The Grants', and the mega-hit 'A&W' all considering her youth, perception and impact.

SAY "YES" TO 'SAY YES TO HEAVEN'

There's nothing a fanbase longs for more than the release of long-rumoured music. 'Say Yes to Heaven' began life as a leaked demo, supposedly for *Ultraviolence*, as early as 2012. Variants were reportedly recorded and cut from future albums, until a leak eventually went viral on TikTok and Lana finally released an official version of the dreamy love ballad.

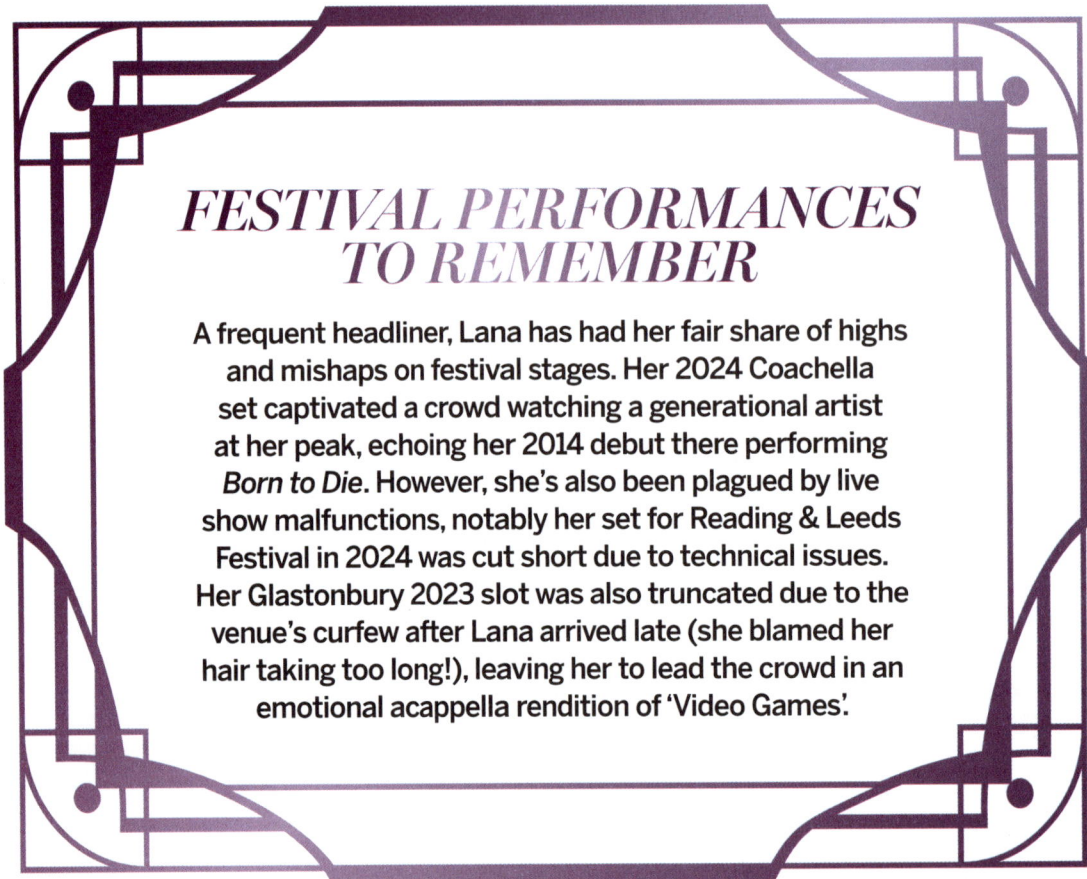

FESTIVAL PERFORMANCES TO REMEMBER

A frequent headliner, Lana has had her fair share of highs and mishaps on festival stages. Her 2024 Coachella set captivated a crowd watching a generational artist at her peak, echoing her 2014 debut there performing *Born to Die*. However, she's also been plagued by live show malfunctions, notably her set for Reading & Leeds Festival in 2024 was cut short due to technical issues. Her Glastonbury 2023 slot was also truncated due to the venue's curfew after Lana arrived late (she blamed her hair taking too long!), leaving her to lead the crowd in an emotional acappella rendition of 'Video Games'.

AN AMERICAN BRIDE

Ever the romantic, Lana surprised the world when she married Jeremy Dufrene in 2024. The pair had met several years ago when Lana went on a wildlife tour on one of his boats. The couple had only been in the public eye for a brief period before their wedding photos emerged: a sweet and intimate ceremony in Dufrene's hometown in Louisiana.

A DECORATED CAREER

Unsurprisingly given her commercial and widespread critical success, Lana Del Rey has picked up countless award nominations through her career. Among her many trophies, she is regularly cited as one of the most impactful artists of the generation. Her influence on pop's landscape is undeniable, bringing darker sounds, fully rounded concepts, poetic lyricism and nostalgia-tinged genre-blending to the fore.

THE RIGHT PERSON WILL STAY

Lana announced her 2025 album, *The Right Person Will Stay*, in an Instagram post detailing a few of its contributors, including longtime collaborator Jack Antonoff and country artist Luke Laird. Originally announced under the title *Lasso*, Lana told *NME* the record would have more country and Americana leanings, and be more melody focused rather than strictly self-revealing. At the time of writing, Lana has recently teased the record's upcoming lead single, 'Henry, Come On'.

THE 2025 TOUR

We know Lana loves Americana, but she is also a big fan of performing across the pond. Indeed, her 2025 plans include a stadium tour across the UK and Ireland. Playing in front of thousands of fans each night – including two sell-out shows at Wembley Stadium – this will be her first-ever stadium tour across the British Isles. Before the year even began, Lana became the highest-selling solo act of 2025 in the UK and Ireland when her tour tickets were eagerly snapped up.

Activities

Tick off the ones you've done!

Images Getty Images. Illustration Kym Winters

Quiz

Easy

It's time to put your Lana knowledge to the test!
How many answers to each level do you know?

1. What is Lana's real name?
- [ ] Elizabeth Woolridge Grant
- [ ] Stefani Joanne Germanotta
- [ ] Ella Yelich-O'Connor
- [ ] Katheryn Hudson

2. Which state was she born in?
- [ ] Florida
- [ ] California
- [ ] New York
- [ ] Oklahoma

3. What was Lana's debut single?
- [ ] 'High by the Beach'
- [ ] 'Love'
- [ ] 'Doin' Time'
- [ ] 'Video Games'

4. Complete the title of Lana's 2011 breakthrough album:
Born to ___
- [ ] *Cry*
- [ ] *Lie*
- [ ] *Die*
- [ ] *Sigh*

5. 'Snow on the Beach' is a duet between Lana and which artist?
- [ ] Taylor Swift
- [ ] Father John Misty
- [ ] Billie Eilish
- [ ] Lorde

6. Which Baz Luhrmann film includes 'Young and Beautiful'?
- [ ] *Romeo + Juliet*
- [ ] *The Great Gatsby*
- [ ] *Moulin Rouge*
- [ ] *Elvis*

7. Lana's originally announced *The Right Person Will Stay* under which country-themed title?
- [ ] *Yee-Haw*
- [ ] *Howdy*
- [ ] *Lasso*
- [ ] *Yippee-Ki-Yay!*

8. Lana's 2023 Glastonbury show was cut short after she arrived late. What reason did she give for her tardiness?
- [ ] She was stuck in traffic
- [ ] She got lost
- [ ] Her hair took too long
- [ ] Her phone was set to the wrong time zone

9. Which of the following Lana songs features The Weeknd?
- [ ] 'Shades of Cool'
- [ ] 'Lust for Life'
- [ ] 'West Coast'
- [ ] 'Cinnamon Girl'

10. Which of the following is NOT a Lana Del Rey album?
- [ ] *Lust for Life*
- [ ] *Ultraviolence*
- [ ] *Honeymoon*
- [ ] *Melancholia*

You can find the answers to each quiz level on page 96.

Quiz
Medium

1. How many words are there in Lana's longest album title?

   _____

2. Which Fleetwood Mac member collaborated with Lana on 'Beautiful People Beautiful Problems'?
   - ☐ Stevie Nicks
   - ☐ Christine McVie
   - ☐ Mick Fleetwood
   - ☐ Lindsey Buckingham

3. The title of her sixth album includes a reference to which painter and illustrator?

   _____

4. One of Lana's songs has TWO famous music festivals in its title – which ones?
   - ☐ Glastonbury
   - ☐ Coachella
   - ☐ Lollapalooza
   - ☐ Woodstock

5. Which cut album track did Lana eventually release in 2023 after it went viral on TikTok?

   _____

6. What colour are the titular banisters of Lana's eighth album?
   - ☐ Green
   - ☐ Violet
   - ☐ Blue
   - ☐ Black

7. Which seasonal emotion sleeper hit is Lana's longest-charting single on the *Billboard* Hot 100?

   _____

8. *Lost at Sea* – a 2023 piano album featuring Lana on vocals – was released by…
   - ☐ Her father
   - ☐ Her mother
   - ☐ Her sister
   - ☐ Her brother

9. Lana has won prestigious Ivor Novello awards for her songwriting

   ☐ True   ☐ False

10. 'Don't Call Me Angel' for *Charlie's Angels* featured Lana and which TWO other artists?
    - ☐ Ariana Grande
    - ☐ Beyoncé
    - ☐ Miley Cyrus
    - ☐ Shakira

QUIZ
Expert

1. When is Lana's birthday?

_____

2. Which track was nominated for Song of the Year at the 2024 Grammys?
- [ ] 'Margaret
- [ ] 'Breaking Up Slowly'
- [ ] 'Let the Light In'
- [ ] 'A&W'

3. Which British football team does she support?

_____

4. Which subject did Lana major in at college?
- [ ] Philosophy
- [ ] Literature
- [ ] Theatre Studies
- [ ] Fine Arts

5. Lana released TWO studio albums in 2021, which were they?

_____

_____

6. Which of these Lana events DIDN'T happen in 2024?
- [ ] She got married
- [ ] Headlined Reading & Leeds Festival
- [ ] Headlined Coachella
- [ ] Released her poetry book

7. What is the title of Lana's 2020 poetry book?

_____

_____

8. Who is Lana's husband?

_____

9. How many octaves does Lana's vocal range span?
- [ ] One
- [ ] Three
- [ ] Five
- [ ] Eight

10. Lana's younger sister Caroline is mentioned in several songs, but under what nickname?

_____

Check your answers on page 96.

*Word*search

Can you find the Lana albums in the jumble below?

```
B  W  O  N  K  U  O  Y  D  I  D  N  B  D  H
O  I  Y  P  U  F  N  J  T  O  K  O  L  W  E
R  O  E  E  H  T  Z  S  T  V  I  S  U  C  C
N  X  R  Z  L  F  F  M  F  R  X  R  E  R  N
T  B  L  N  J  M  U  E  T  F  N  E  B  L  E
O  C  E  A  B  R  S  J  R  N  N  P  A  U  L
D  S  D  G  U  I  H  S  N  B  X  T  N  S  O
I  S  A  Z  R  M  B  O  W  Z  M  H  I  T  I
E  U  N  F  J  I  O  H  J  N  Q  G  S  F  V
R  E  A  T  B  M  A  X  W  D  H  I  T  O  A
E  H  L  F  Y  R  D  G  D  Y  X  R  E  R  R
J  A  X  E  M  K  I  A  C  E  A  V  R  L  T
Y  I  N  V  Z  C  Z  X  C  C  O  O  S  I  L
F  O  J  S  L  I  A  R  T  M  E  H  C  F  U
H  P  J  Q  F  B  Z  S  I  T  R  Z  C  E  Q
```

Find these words...

BORNTODIE	LUSTFORLIFE	BLUEBANISTERS
ULTRAVIOLENCE	NFR	DIDYOUKNOW
HONEYMOON	CHEMTRAILS	RIGHTPERSON

Inspiration MAZE

Check your route on page 97.

Lana's going for a drive to help spark ideas for new songs – can you find the route to her next big hit?

Design an OUTFIT

Create your own unique Lana look for the next red carpet event

Crossword

Use your knowledge of Lana's lyrics to fill in the blanks and solve this puzzle

DOWN

1. "If you weren't mine I'd be ___ of your love" • 'Venice Bitch' (7)

2. "They mistook my kindness for ___" • 'Mariners Apartment Complex' (8)

4. "He plays ___ while I sing Lou Reed" • 'Brooklyn Baby' (6)

5. "Something about the way he says, 'Don't ___ me'" • 'Did You Know...' (6)

6. "Be my undercover ___, babe" • 'Summer Bummer' (5)

7. "Come take a walk on the ___" • 'Born to Die' (4,4)

11. "Cause we're the masters of our own ___" • 'Lust for Life' (4)

12. "God knows I begged, begged, ___ and cried" • 'God Knows I Tried' (8)

13. "It's all for ___" • 'Video Games' (3)

17. "Me and my friends, we miss ___" • 'The Greatest' (4,1,4)

18. "I've got my ___" • 'Say Yes to Heaven' (3,2,3)

19. "I haven't done a ___ since I was nine" • 'A&W' (9)

23. "He makes me shine like ___" • 'Young and Beautiful' (8)

25. "I get down to beat ___" • 'Brooklyn Baby' (6)

ACROSS

3. "Don't leave, I just need a ___ call" • 'The Greatest' (4,2)

8. "Said he'd fix my weathervane, give me ___, take away my pain" • 'Blue Banisters' (8)

9. "Telephone wires above are sizzlin' ___" • 'Summertime Sadness' (4,1,5)

10. "You get ready, you get all ___ up". • 'Love' (7)

12. "I just wanted you to know that, ___, you the best" • 'Summertime Sadness' (4)

14. "I'm not unhinged or unhappy, I'm just ___" • 'Chemtrails over the Country Club' (4)

15. "Don't ask if I'm ___, you know that I'm not" • 'Hope Is a Dangerous Thing...' (5)

16. "I hear the birds on the ___" • 'Ride' (6,6)

20. "My boyfriend's ___ and he's cooler than ever" • 'Lust for Life' (4)

21. "You want in, but you just can't ___" • 'Art Deco' (3)

22. "Nothing ___ can stay" • 'Venice Bitch' (4)

24. "You were sorta punk rock, I grew up on ___" • 'Blue Jeans' (3,3)

26. "___ is the anthem of success" • 'National Anthem' (5)

27. "They say that the ___ was built for two" • 'Video Games' (5)

Lyrics by Lana Del Rey & collaborators (Jack Antonoff, Jordan Carter, Sam Dew, Andrew Joseph Gradwohl Jr, Emilie Haynie, Mike Hermosa, Benjamin Levin, Max Martin, Rakim Mayers, Rick Nowels, Barrie O'Neill, Justin Parker, Matthew Samuels, Gabe Simon, Jahaan Sweet, Abel Tesfaye, The Nexus, Tyler Williams)

Check your answers on page 97.

ANAGRAMS

Can you unscramble the words below to find the Lana song titles?

1. ARIACAD

2. REDCOAT

3. DARTBEREN

4. NILROMANCING

5. PARKASRAIDED

6. DIMETONI

7. REPSIFTING

8. TARGETTHESE

9. MONEYOHNO

10. DISPARATEWHOOP

11. FLIMSYENGINE

12. SUITKING

13. UNLOCKYES

14. RAGETRAM

15. DEMOONLY

16. OVALTEARS

17. UNCLEARVIOLET

18. OMEGADIVES

19. TACOSWETS

20. WARHEADTILT

WORDOKUS

Fill in the blank squares so that each row, column and sub-grid contains every letter of the target word given on the right

EASY
WORD: CARMEN

C		R	M	E	
	N		R		
M	E	A		R	C
		N	E	A	
	R	C	A	M	
A			E		N

MEDIUM
WORD: OCEANBLVD

	V		N	A	B			O
		L	C	D				V
A	O	N			L			
	N		O		E	C		A
		A	N		B			
L		B	D		C			N
	E		L			N		B
			C	V	D			
B		C	E	O	N		A	L

HARD
WORD: CHEMTRAIL

L			I	A	E			H
C	H			T	R			
	R	A		C		T		E
		C		L		H		M
	T		A		C			R
M		L		H		C	A	
E				I		M	C	
		H					E	A
A	I	H	C	E		L		T

Check your answers on page 97.

Can you find the 8 changes made to the image on the right?

SPOT THE

Check your
answers on
page 97.

DIFFERENCE

ANSWERS

QUIZZES

Easy

1. Elizabeth Woolridge Grant
2. New York
3. 'Video Games'
4. Die
5. Taylor Swift
6. *The Great Gatsby*
7. *Lasso*
8. Her hair took too long
9. 'Lust for Life'
10. *Melancholia*

Medium

1. 10 words: *Did You Know That There's a Tunnel Under Ocean Blvd*
2. Stevie Nicks
3. Norman Rockwell
4. Coachella and Woodstock
5. 'Say Yes to Heaven'
6. Blue
7. 'Summertime Sadness'
8. Her father
9. True
10. Ariana Grande and Miley Cyrus

Expert

1. 21 June 1985
2. 'A&W'
3. Liverpool Football Club
4. Philosophy
5. *Chemtrails over the Country Club* and *Blue Banisters*
6. Released her poetry book
7. *Violet Bent Backwards over the Grass*
8. Jeremy Dufrene
9. Three
10. Chuck or Chucky

Quiz answers correct as of March 2025

WORDSEARCH

Secret answer!

MAZE

START

FINISH

CROSSWORD

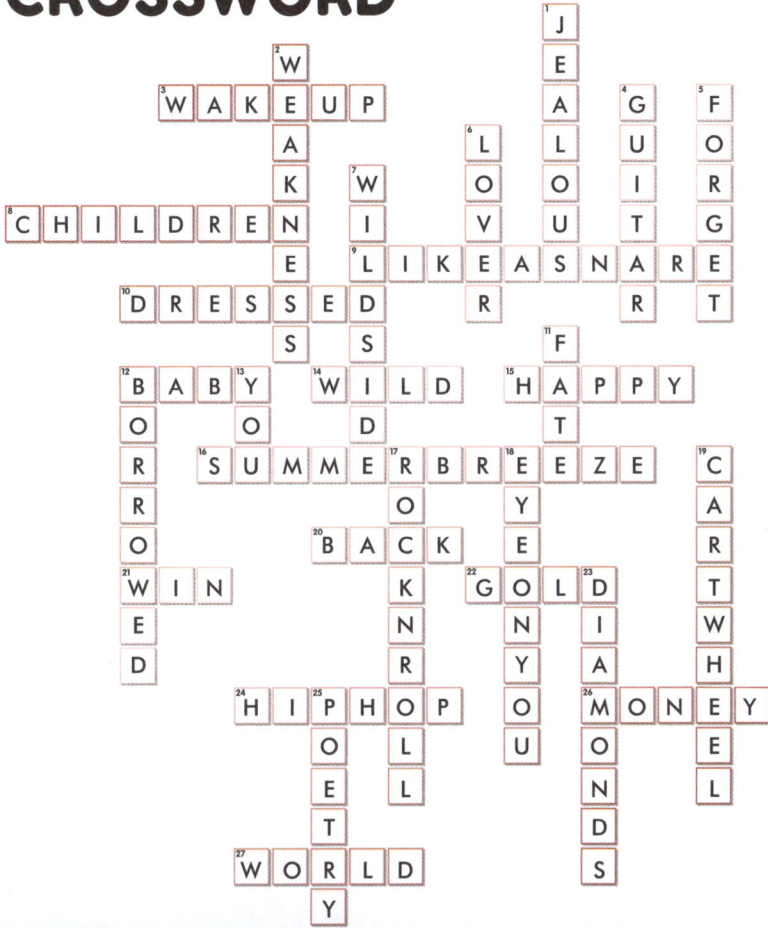

ANAGRAMS

1. ARCADIA
2. ART DECO
3. BARTENDER
4. CINNAMON GIRL
5. DARK PARADISE
6. DOIN TIME
7. FINGERTIPS
8. THE GREATEST
9. HONEYMOON
10. HOW TO DISAPPEAR
11. IN MY FEELINGS
12. KINTSUGI
13. LUCKY ONES
14. MARGARET
15. OLD MONEY
16. SALVATORE
17. ULTRAVIOLENCE
18. VIDEO GAMES
19. WEST COAST
20. WILD AT HEART

SPOT THE DIFFERENCE

WORDOKUS

EASY
WORD: CARMEN

MEDIUM
WORD: OCEANBLVD

HARD
WORD: CHEMTRAIL